THE DEWEY DECIMAL SYSTEM

A TRUE BOOK
by
Allan Fowler

Children's Press®
A Division of Grolier Publishing

New York London Hong Kong Sydney
Danbury, Connecticut

Reading Consultant
Linda Cornwell
*Learning Resource
Consultant
Indiana Department of
Education*

Use of the Dewey Decimal
System can help you find
any book you want to read
in the library.

Library of Congress Cataloging-in-Publication Data

Fowler, Allan.
  The Dewey decimal sytem / by Allan Fowler
    p. cm. — (A True book)
  Includes index.
Summary: Explains how the Dewey decimal system of classification for
libraries was invented and how it works.
    ISBN 0-516-20132-8 (lib.bdg.)   ISBN 0-516-26130-4 (pbk.)
    1. Classification, Dewey decimal—Juvenile literature.
[1. Classification, Dewey decimal.] I. Title II. Series.
Z696.D7F65 1996
025.4'31—dc20   96-13870
                                                        CIP
                                                        AC

Contents

Do you have lots of books at home? How do you keep track of them?

Sorting Out the Books

Do you have a lot of books at home? How about at school? If you have more books than you can keep track of, then you have some idea of the problems facing the people in charge of libraries. Every librarian needs a way of knowing the title of every book in the library and where each book is. A public library may have many millions of books, but it should still be easy for readers to find any book they want.

A list of the books in a library is called a "catalog" (sometimes spelled catalogue). Even the oldest known libraries had catalogs. Libraries today organize their books either on index cards or in a computer database. In

This reader used the catalog to find a book.

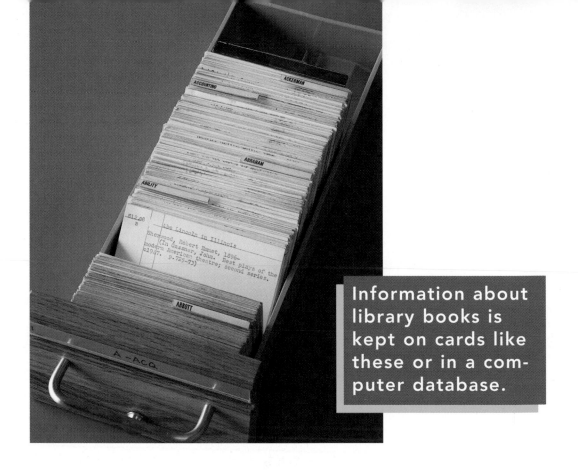

Information about library books is kept on cards like these or in a computer database.

the past, books were grouped according to their subject matter—what the books were about. But people had different ways of doing this, so that method was confusing.

Today it's easy to find a specific book on a library's shelves, or to find several books on the same subject, or to find many books by one author. It's easy because a practical system for organizing books was invented by Melvil Dewey, who lived from 1851 to 1931. More than anyone else, Dewey developed the librarian's job into a skilled profession.

Melvil Dewey and Amherst College, where Dewey went to school

Dewey began planning his system while he was still a student at Amherst College, Massachusetts. In 1876, he finished creating the system, which is now known as the Dewey Decimal System. It is still used by thousands of school and public libraries today.

Melvil Dewey went on to establish the first school for training librarians, at Columbia College in New York City. He was also a founder of the American Library Association.

Most public libraries use the Dewey Decimal System.

How the System Works

How does the Dewey
Decimal System work? You
can think of it like a code
that uses numbers. Each
book is put in a certain group
and is given a three-digit
number, depending on its

type or subject. A digit is one number, 0 through 9, that is part of a bigger number. (For instance, 2 is the first digit in the number 245, and 4 is the second digit.) The first digit of the three-digit Dewey Decimal number tells you what main Dewey group a book belongs to. On the following pages are the ten basic Dewey categories and their number groups.

The Dewey Categories

ere are the ten basic Dewey categories:

000 Reference works—encyclopedias,
newspapers, magazines

100 Philosophy and pyschology

200 Religion

300 Social sciences—law, education,
customs, everyday life

400 Languages

500 Basic sciences—mathematics, chemistry

600 Applied sciences—technology, medicine,
engineering

700 The arts—architecture, painting, music

800 Literature—
poetry,
novels, plays

900 Geography,
biography,
and history

The writings of the great philosopher Socrates (right) are kept in the 100s section in the library.

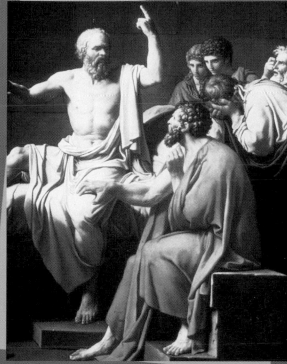

Louis Pasteur's (left) scientific works can be found in the 500s section.

To read the literature of Jane Austen (right), look for books in the 800s. Books about geography (far left) are in the 900s, but may also be shelved with the reference books.

Categories such as "basic sciences" or "the arts" cover a lot of ground. So each main group is broken down into ten specific subject areas. The second digit of a book's Dewey number tells you to which subdivision it belongs. Then the third digit provides even more specific information about the book's subject matter. Additional digits after a decimal point narrow it down even more. (A decimal point looks just like the period at the end of this sentence.)

A label is made for each book. It shows the Dewey number and the first three letters of the author's last name. Sometimes it also shows the letter "J" if it is an adult book that is kept in the children's section. The label is then is put on the book's spine—the part of the book that faces out on the shelf. The spine usually has the

The labels on the books show where they belong on the shelves.

author's name and the book title printed on it. Books are placed on library shelves in order by their Dewey numbers.

What the Numbers Mean

Are you ready for an example? Let's look up "magic" in the library's catalog. Under the subject "magic," books are listed with the Dewey number 793.8. The 700 numbers, as shown in the chart on pages 14–15, are for books on the arts.

To learn this magic trick, you would read books labeled 793.8.

The ten subdivisions of the 700 group are listed on the following pages.

700 The arts (general)
710 Civic and landscape art
720 Architecture
730 Sculpture
740 Decorative arts

To find out about the house called Falling Water (left) and its designer, Frank Lloyd Wright, look in the 720s. The 730s include books about sculpture, such as the *Alice in Wonderland* statue (right) in Central Park, New York.

The 750s section has books on painting, such as *Gabrielle and Jean* by August Renoir (left) and *Afternoon Flight* by Andrew Wyeth (below).

In the 790 group, the number 793 is given to books on games, puzzles, and party fun. But all books on magic should be next to each other on the library shelf. That means they need a number of their own. So another digit was added after the decimal point, giving us 793.8.

Books on board games, such as chess, are shelved with books on sports.

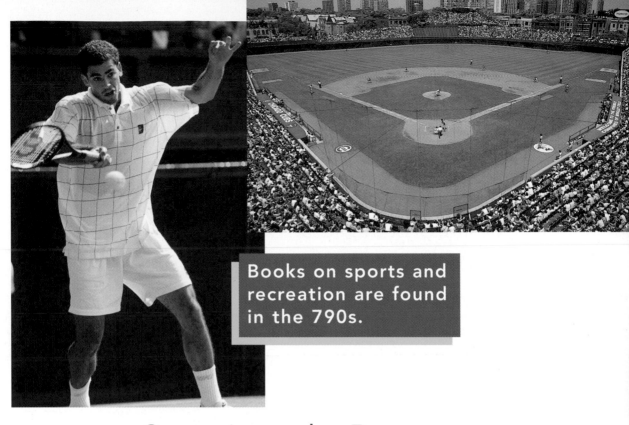

Books on sports and recreation are found in the 790s.

Sometimes the Dewey Decimal system can surprise you. For instance, books on sports and recreation are found in the 790s, but a biography on Pete Sampras might be shelved in the 900s—that's where the biographies are!

A Book and Its Dewey Number

Suppose you want to find the book *When a Storm Comes Up*, by Allan Fowler. In your library's computer, you will see its catalog entry.

Rookie Read-About® Science
When a Storm Comes Up

When a storm comes up

551.55
FOW
Fowler, Allan
   When a storm comes up / by Allan Fowler. - Chicago : Childrens Press, ©1995.

   32 p. : col. ill.   (Rookie read-about science)

   Summary: Examines the weather conditions that produce storms, different kinds of storms, the damage they can cause, and how to find safety from a storm.

   ISBN 0-516-06035-X
   94-35627

   1. Storms I. Title II. Series

                                         551.55
                              QC941.3.F69 1995
                                  Childrens Press

The Dewey number for this title is 551.55. This number begins with 5, because the 500s are basic sciences. To find this book, you would go to the part of the library where the 500s are kept.

On the book's spine, you will see a label that shows the Dewey number and the first three letters of the author's last name.

551.55
FOW

Benefits of the Dewey System

How does the Dewey system make your library visits more fun? First, it helps you find the book you want quickly and easily. You look it up in the card catalog or computer catalog under the book's title or under the author's last

R200.4 A -
R328.73 R

500 T -
550.9 Z

551 A -
581.5 Z

R000 A -
R200.3 Z

Signs are posted to show the different sections in the library. The Dewey system organizes the books, so readers can find them.

name. The listing includes the book's Dewey number, which you write down. The books on the library shelves are lined up in order by number, with their Dewey numbers clearly printed on their spines. When you know the Dewey number, you can find any book you need.

Here's another way the Dewey system helps you. Suppose you would like to read about a certain subject, but you don't know what books the library has on that subject. The Dewey catalog also lists books under their subject. So if you want a biography of the first U.S. president, you look up the listings for "Washington, George." Or "Dinosaurs" or "Basketball" or "Travel—Africa" or whatever interests you. Then you write down the numbers of any books that seem promising. When you

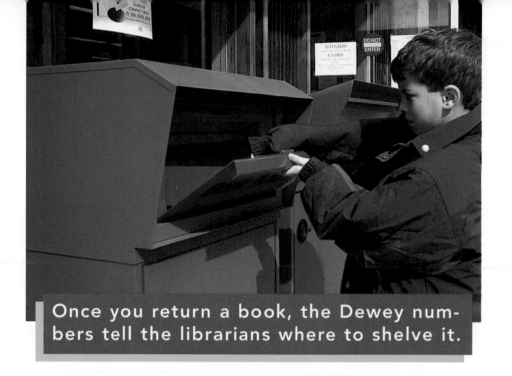

Once you return a book, the Dewey numbers tell the librarians where to shelve it.

When you return a book, its Dewey number tells the librarian which shelf to put it on—so someone else can find it later. Imagine trying to find a book in the library if they didn't have catalog numbers. It might take you longer to find a book than to read it!

920.7
940

Librarians sort the books, place them on carts, and then put them back on the shelves, according to the Dewey numbers.

OTHER
DIVISIONS
RETURN

HERE

Exceptions and Updates

You may see some books on library shelves that are not grouped according to catalog numbers. You will find fiction—novels and short stories—arranged in alphabetical order under their authors' names. Oversized books will be on

Librarians will help
you if you have trouble
finding books.

shelves big enough to hold them. And in some libraries, certain valuable books are set aside, and you have to ask the librarian to get them for you. Reference books—such as encyclopedias, dictionaries, or atlases—may also be kept in a special place.

The Dewey system is not the only one used in libraries today. The Library of Congress—the national library of the United States, in

Washington, D.C.—developed a classification system based on combinations of letters and numbers. Most large public libraries, libraries at

Big libraries at colleges, like this one, use a different system for organizing books.

colleges and universities, and libraries specializing in particular subjects use the Library of Congress system. Most local libraries and school libraries use the Dewey numbers.

But how can a system that was first published in 1876 provide numbers for books about things that didn't even exist back then—such as automobiles, airplanes, space travel, television, and

Dewey numbers are added for new inventions—such as television and space travel.

A Dewey number can be created for any idea you may have.

computers? An organization called the Online Computer Library Center revises the Dewey system about every seven to ten years, giving numbers to new subjects. Since they can add as many digits as they like after the decimal point, the Dewey system is in no danger of running out of numbers.

So even if you come up with a great new idea—like a robot that does your homework for

Reading at home is fun, and the Dewey Decimal System makes it easy to find books you like.

you—and write a book about it, there will be a Dewey number for it. And every kid can find your book in the library.

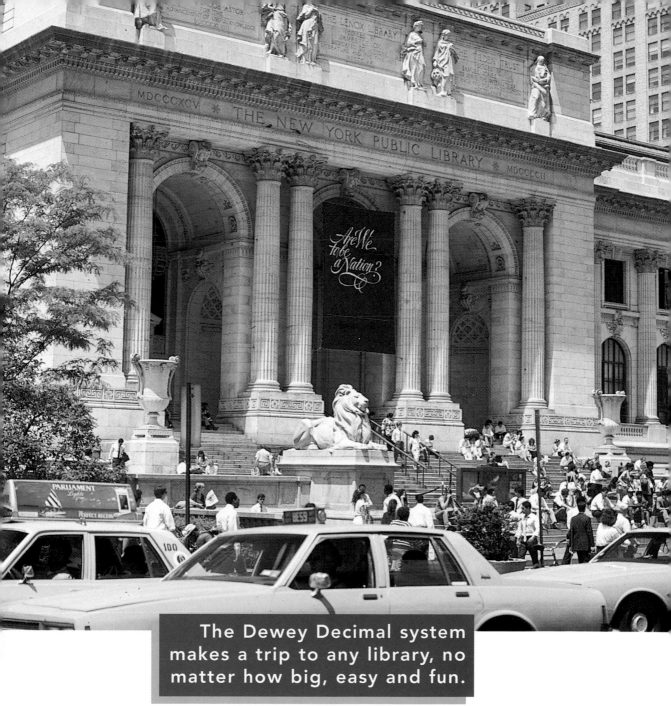

The Dewey Decimal system makes a trip to any library, no matter how big, easy and fun.

43

To Find Out More

Here are some additional resources to help you learn more about the Dewey Decimal system.

 **Books**

 **Organizations**

Fowler, Allan. **The Dewey Decimal System.** Children's Press, 1996.

Gibbons, Gail. **Check It Out! The Book About Libraries.** Harcourt and Brace, 1988.

Knowlton, Jack. Books & **Libraries.** Harper Collins Children's Books, 1991.

Santrey, Laurence. **Using the Library**. Troll Associates, 1985.

American Library Association
50 E. Huron St.
Chicago, IL 60611
312/ 440-9374
e-mail: *pio@ala.org*

Friends of Libraries U.S.A.
1700 Walnut Street
Philadelphia, PA 19103
(215) 790-1674

Library of Congress
Jefferson Building
1st Street, SE
Washington, D.C. 20540
e-mail: *lcweb@loc.gov*

Online Sites

Library of Congress Home Page
http.//www.loc.gov.

Information on the Library's collections and exhibits.

Library of Congress Online System (LOCIS)
http://lcweb.loc.gov./home-page/online.html

The Library's collection of databases.

National Digital Learning Program
http://www.lcweb2.loc.gov./ammem/ndlpedu/index.html

A varied collection of online learning resources.

Events and Exhibits
http://lcweb.loc.gov./home-page/event.html

Learn about ongoing exhibits and upcoming events.

Historical Text Archive
http://www.msstate.edu/Archives/History

Explore historical documents, photographs, and diaries from many countries and time periods.

Important Words

architecture the art of designing buildings

catalog a complete list of items, given in a special order

database a large collection of information, usually in a computer

decimal being numbered by ten. Also means a decimal point, which looks like the period at the end of this sentence

digit any number, 0 through 9, that makes up a larger number

graphic arts writing or printing that includes symbols

recreation hobbies, including sports and games

sculpture the process of making three-dimensional pieces of art, such as statues

social sciences the study of everyday life and how people live together

Index

Meet the Author

Allan Fowler is a free-lance writer with a background in advertising. Born in New York, he now lives in Chicago and enjoys traveling.